The 2019 Guide to Pricing Your Photography

By

Anthony Morganti

Copyright © 2018 by Anthony Morganti

All rights reserved. No part of this publication may be reproduced, distributed, or transmitted in any form or by any means, including photocopying, recording, or other electronic or mechanical methods, without the prior written permission of the author, except in the case of brief quotations embodied in critical reviews and certain other noncommercial uses permitted by copyright law.

For permission requests, email the author at: Tony@AnthonyMorganti.com

Table of Contents

INTRODUCTION 4

PART ONE - HOW TO PRICE 6

    Types of Professional Photography 7
    Being a Business Person 9
    Cost of Business 11
    Negotiating Principles 15
    Rights & Copyright 17

PART TWO - REAL LIFE PRICING STORIES 19

PART THREE - 2019 PHOTOGRAPHY PRICING 23

    Band Photography 24
    Birthing Sessions 26
    Boudoir 28
    Concert Photography 30
    Corporate Photography 32
    Engagement Sessions 33
    Event Photography 35
    Fine Art 37
    General Portraiture 43
    Magazine Photography 45
    Mini Sessions 47
    Newborns 48
    Photojournalism 50
    Prom Photography 53
    School Pictures 55
    Seniors 57
    Social Media Photography 60
    Sports Teams 62
    Weddings 65
    Add To Order 68

DID YOU LIKE THE 2019 GUIDE TO PRICING YOUR PHOTOGRAPHY? 75

ABOUT THE AUTHOR 76

Introduction

One of the hardest decisions a professional photographer has to make is how much they should charge for their work. Often we're afraid of setting our prices too high fearing that potential customers will go to the cheaper photographer yet, we're also mindful of setting our prices too low because who wants to earn less than what is possible?

In Part 1 of this book, I will help you set your pricing but more importantly, this guide will help you determine your cost of doing business, help you realize the value of your time, learn how competitive your market is, and assist you in setting pricing that will make you a fair profit and ultimately, a comfortable living.

Once you have a firm understanding of all those things, you'll be better able to confidently set your pricing knowing that you're not pricing yourself out of your market and you're not leaving any money on the table.

In Part 2 of this book, you'll read some stories from photographers about how they came about setting their pricing — what they did that worked as well as what they did that didn't work.

Finally, in Part 3 of this book, you'll find recommended pricing for several different types of photography. Parts 1 and 2 of this book gave you insight on how to determine what you need to do to be profitable. This, of course, will be different for everyone. Some photographers will have more overhead or cost of doing business. Others will have bigger families to house, feed, and clothe and finally, others may be working in a more competitive market. You will pick the type of photography and the level within that type that will cover your overhead, feed, clothe, and house your family, and, make you a fair competitor in your market.

The pricing levels will vary by type of photography — some might include pricing for, *Beginner*, *Intermediate*, and *Expert* photographers while others will be grouped by the potential distribution of the image. For example, you'll get more money if you sell pictures to *Time Magazine* than you will if you sell the same photos to the *Paducah Sun*. The prices in this manual are meant to be guides to help you set your pricing. You can, of course, charge a different amount than the amounts listed. You need to have a good reason to do so. Some of those reasons are:

- The market you're in is saturated with photographers so you'll need to charge less than the *Low* listed amount. Conversely, if you're the only photographer in town and the town is relatively affluent, you may be able to charge more than the *High* amount listed.

- You're a relative beginner and do not have an extensive portfolio to show. You can keep your prices lower than *Low* until you build up your portfolio and get clientele. I caution you when doing this. You'll probably find that you won't have to go lower than the *Low* listed price to get customers despite your relative newness to the profession.

- You're the best photographer in the area, and everyone that is anyone in your town insists on having you as their photographer. In those cases, you should charge what your talent demands even if it's more than the *High* pricing listed in this guide.

Without further ado, let's get started!

Part One - How to Price

I have this book divided into three parts. In this, Part One, I'll discuss some things concerning the business of photography that you should be aware. Most importantly, I'll be talking about the cost of doing business, and I'll be explaining *Rights* and *Copyright.*

The business of photography has had sweeping changes over the past several years. The advent of digital and the lower relative cost of equipment has swamped the market with "Photographers".

What I mean by that is that nowadays, almost everyone has a smartphone and with it, they're taking pictures every day. Although phone photography isn't technically up to the professional level yet, what is happening is that more people than ever are being exposed to the beauty of photography, and gaining an interest in it, that they likely wouldn't have garnered had they not been doing it so often with their cell phone. With more people interested in photography because of their phone, more people are upgrading — buying more sophisticated cameras such as DSLR's and mirrorless systems. They're taking better pictures and sooner or later, someone tells them, "You should do this professionally" and wallah! A professional photographer is born.

There are more professional photographers today than there ever has been and the competition is keen. Unfortunately, far too many aren't competent enough to stay in business long but, for every one that flames out, two more are there to take their place.

What about the new professional that is competent? The photographer that is producing great work and developing a client base — how can that photographer navigate pricing to not only get work but to make a profit in today's competitive marketplace?

I believe, a thorough understanding of the market coupled with a basic knowledge of business should be enough to help today's professional make a profit from every job, and a living doing what they love. It is my opinion that most business books complicate things and most pricing guides aren't realistic. In this guide, I'm going to take a more simplistic business approach touching on the things that I think, from a business perspective, you should be aware of. Then, when I do list pricing, you'll have a better idea if the prices I list accurately reflect your market and if you can make a living doing a specific type of photography.

Types of Professional Photography

There are dozens if not hundreds of different types of professional photography. In this book, I'm going to cover the pricing of twenty popular types of professional photography. Included are:

- Band Photography
- Birthing Sessions
- Boudoir
- Concert Photography
- Corporate Photography
- Engagement Sessions
- Event Photography
- Fine Art (Print Sales)
- General Portraiture
- Magazine Photography
- Mini Sessions
- Newborn Photography
- Photojournalism
- Prom Photography
- School Pictures
- Senior Photography
- Social Media Influencer Photography
- Sport Team Photography
- Wedding Photography
- Add-Ons (Single Print & Product Sales)

Each of these categories presents unique challenges which I explain before the pricing is given. Some of them, such as *Magazine Photography*, are seeing fees plummeting whereas others, such as *Wedding Photography*, are seeing moderate price increases. Many pricing fluctuations are year to year while others are decade to decade. Because of that, you, the professional photographer, must keep your ear to the rail so you're prepared and protected from any adverse changes, and conversely, you're positioned to take advantage of any positive changes in the industry.

Being a Business Person

I began my professional photography career, 40-years ago, as a wedding photographer. I quickly came to realize that the actual picture taking part of the job was the smallest part. I would spend, on average, 8-hours taking photographs during a wedding. Leading up to that was me meeting with prospective clients, explaining the packages available and the contract. Accepting deposits and writing receipts. After the wedding I got the images processed, sorted and numbered negatives (which took hours), printed the proofs then arranged and assembled proof books. Then I would meet with my clients, explain the proof to print process and describe the products available then take their order. Next, I would order the albums, print the pictures, assemble the albums and frame pictures that needed framing. I would then deliver the product and often take subsequent orders and do the print, framing, and meeting with the client part of it again.

When I wasn't meeting with clients, I was doing bookkeeping, huddling with my accountant, and meeting with other professionals in the wedding industry such as bridal gown stores and reception venues.

Realistically, I estimate for every 8-hours of picture taking; I worked another 40-60 hours on everything else. When I began, I naively thought that if I charged $2000.00 for a wedding and, after material costs, walked away with $1600.00, I earned, $200.00 an hour. I quickly came to realize that after working at a minimum of 48-hours on that wedding, my hourly pay shrunk to $33.33 an hour.

That $33.33 an hour still sounds good, doesn't it? Well, I left out a lot of stuff. I accounted for the cost of the prints, wedding albums, and the frames but what about my other work-related expenses. Here are some of my business bills I paid back then, estimated for that 48-hour period in 1978:

Studio Rent:	$100.00
Vehicle Maintenance & Gas:	$50.00
Business Insurance:	$22.00
Utilities & Phone:	$30.00
Equipment Depreciation:	$10.00
Advertising:	$25.00
Professional Association Fees:	$8.00

Total business cost for that 48-hour period: $245.00

That causes my hourly pay to shrink to $28.22 — still not too bad for 1978! But, wait a minute. I didn't account for my taxes. Since I was self-employed, I was taxed at the higher self-employment tax rate of 27%. That left me with $989.15 earned over that 48-hour period of work — $20.60 an hour.

So, I had to work a minimum of 48-hours a week earning at best, $20.60 an hour with which, I had to pay my personal bills and feed and clothe myself and my wife. During that time I was also going to college full-time along with my wife. Later, we had the burden of student loans and a bit later, the joy and cost associated with a child.

That was a lot of work for $20.60 an hour, and the truth is, I almost always, for the week, worked more than 48-hours for that same, $2000.00 check.

When you price out your services, you must have an accurate idea of what your cost of doing business is as well as what your cost of living is. Without knowing both, you're figuratively, shooting in the dark.

Cost of Business

In any business, you need to know how much it will cost you to be in business before you can price any of your products or services. When a photographer turns professional, he or she will have a lot of seemingly unrelated expenses that must be accounted for. It can be very complicated accounting for every nickel and dime — I hope to cut through the confusion by sharing with you what has worked for me.

I try to keep things as simple as possible, and when I started to get very busy, I created a spreadsheet to help me understand what my business expenses were and what I needed to bill out to make ends meet. Later, when looking at spreadsheets created by other professionals, I came to realize that mine was simpler and to me, simpler is better, as long as it gets the job done.

You're welcomed to have my spreadsheet to use for yourself. Just go to my website and download it — free, no strings attached:

https://OnlinePhotographyTraining.com/spreadsheet

I'm going to explain the entries in my spreadsheet and what you'll need to know to use it. It's broken down into two input sections, Income, and Expenses and in each field, you should enter your estimated MONTHLY numbers.

The third section, Results, are the calculations of your overhead.

Even if you don't want to use my spreadsheet, you should understand the following and how it will impact your business.

Income

Monthly Income - Your desired gross pay, per month -- this is the amount of money you need to gross, per month, to live.

Number of Days Billed Per Month - This isn't the number of days you work per month -- this is the actual number of days that you write out a bill or receipt and receive pay. For example, a wedding photographer might work four (4) weddings per month so they would put 4 in this field. If you're a portrait photographer that works 5-days a week, you will put 20 here.

Expenses

Studio/Office Rent - I label it as rent on the spreadsheet but if you own the building, this would be your mortgage, taxes, etc. — whatever you pay a month to be in that space.

Photo/Video Equipment & Accessories - If you buy a new camera every year and a couple of new backgrounds, a half a dozen filters, a million batteries — whatever equipment you buy during the year, estimate the monthly amount of all these purchases and put that amount here. Estimate on the higher side because sometimes we all get GAS (Gear Acquisition Syndrome).

Computer Software & Hardware - Do you buy a computer every two years? Have monthly software subscriptions to Adobe and Microsoft? Purchase, outright, a software package once a year? Estimate your monthly cost for all of that and put that figure here.

Web Hosting & Advertising - I lumped this together because to me, my website, is advertising. Whatever you pay for web hosting and any other advertising and promotion, per month, should be put here.

Office Supplies - Stamps, pens, desks, coffee, that squishy nerve calming thing you keep at your desk, etc. Those monthly costs go here.

Phone (Cell & Landline) - Estimated Monthly cost(s).

Utilities - Estimated Monthly cost(s).

Internet Access - Monthly cost.

Business Insurance - Monthly cost for equipment loss and business liability insurance.

Heath Insurance - Monthly cost for health insurance for you and any employees.

Licenses - Any licensing costs go here.

Subscriptions & Professional Dues - Not to be confused with software subscriptions which should go under Software & Hardware. Here you'll put any subscriptions to magazines, websites, and professional organizations that help you further your career and business.

Professional Development - You can lump this together with Subscriptions & Professional dues, but here, you can put a monthly amount for any seminar and workshops you attend. I keep this separate because I'll include travel costs here because I often have to travel to another city to participate in a workshop or seminar.

Vehicle Expenses - Lease, Loan, Insurance, Maintenance, Gas - Estimate this cost per month.

Legal & Accounting Services - Estimated Monthly cost(s).

Employee Costs - This entry might be a little tricky. If you have a regular payroll employee on staff, you must put here not only their monthly gross pay but also add to it the business taxes you pay on their behalf. In the United States, an employer also contributes to their employee's Social Security and Medicare so you'd put in this field your employee's monthly gross pay and add to that, the monthly amount you contribute to their Social Security and Medicare.

If you hire an assistant or second shooter as an outside contractor, you'll merely need to put an average monthly amount you pay them here.

Business & Self Employment Tax - You may need to check with your accountant for a figure to put in this field. Any taxes you pay for your business, go here. Do not put any personal taxes here. Personal taxes come out of your gross pay.

Results

Once you enter your income and expense numbers, the spreadsheet will return a number of results that should help you better understand what you need to earn to not only cover your business expenses but also cover your income (salary).

Total Monthly Expenses - This is the total of all of your expenses for the month.

Total Monthly Expenses Plus Monthly Income - This is the total of all of your expenses for the month and your salary for the month.

Total Yearly Expenses - This is the total of all of your expenses for the year.

Total Yearly Expenses Plus Yearly Income - This is the total of all of your expenses for the year and your salary for the year.

Weekly Cost of Doing Business to Cover Expenses - This is how much money you must earn per week to cover your business expenses for one (1) week.

Weekly Cost of Doing Business to Cover Expenses & Income - This is how much money you must earn per week to cover your business expenses and your income (salary) for one (1) week.

Overhead Cost to Cover Expenses Per Billed Business Day - This takes the number of days you bill per month and returns a minimum amount that you must charge, per billing day, to cover your expenses.

Overhead Cost to Cover Expenses & Income Per Billed Business Day - This takes the number of days you bill per month and returns a minimum amount that you must charge, per billing day, to cover your expenses and your income (salary).

I'm the first to admit that the spreadsheet, cosmetically, isn't the prettiest in the world so feel free to gussy it up to make it look better and change or add entries so that the spreadsheet better fits your business.

The main thing I hope the spreadsheet helps you with is giving you a quantitative understanding of how much money you'll need to earn per billed day, per week, per month, and per year so that your photography business is thriving.

Negotiating Principles

There will come a time when you'll need to negotiate with a client. The difference between being a good negotiator and a bad negotiator can make or break your business, so it's important to learn how to negotiate properly.

There's a bit of art and a lot more science to negotiation which would take up an entire book. There are many books on the subject. In this guide, I'll touch on some significant points. If you want to learn more about the art of negotiations, I suggest you read this book:

Never Split the Difference: Negotiating As If Your Life Depended On It by Chris Voss with Tahl Raz

That book is a bit expensive. If you cannot afford it, I can offer you some tips that should help you better negotiate with a client.

Don't hesitate to ask for what you want - Simply state what your fee is. Make sure that you say it confidently, unapologetically, and clearly. If your client senses the least bit of uneasiness in your voice or your demeanor, this will be a cue for them to attack your pricing and it's validity. Relating to the previous chapter, knowing your overhead and how much it costs you, every day, to be in business, will better equip you mentally, to confidently, unapologetically, and clearly, state your fee.

Don't talk too much - One negotiating ploy is to say as few words as possible and allow your opponent to talk. The more you talk, the more apt you are to say something that will enable an opening for your client to counter your offer.

Shut-up and listen - This goes hand in hand with what I said above. Just state your price and let your client talk and note their reaction and demeanor as they speak. When they're done talking, stay silent — this will usually cue them to speak more. The more they talk, the more apt they'll say something that will give you the opportunity to justify your pricing.

Don't give anything away without getting something in return - You quoted them for 3-hours of photography, but they want 4. Tell them you can do 4, but it will cost x-dollars more. Don't just say, "Okay, I'll do the job for 4-hours." Admittedly, this won't always be possible but, never give anything away without first trying to get something in return, and secondly, know that if you do give it away, that the job will still be profitable.

Explain to the person how their needs will be met - Simply explain how you can do exactly what they want when they want it done.

Don't be in a hurry - Don't rush through the negotiation. As I stated, listen more than you speak and when you do talk, talk slowly and clearly.

Don't be afraid to walk away - This might be the most challenging thing to do. You're so close to getting the job but, yet so far. If the client's demands are unreasonable for any reason, walk away confident that you'll get a better job, paying you your full worth.

Rights & Copyright

It is crucial that any photographer, not just a professional photographer, understand what Copyright and Rights mean. These are two different things, and you should understand them intimately.

Copyright

We'll discuss Copyright first — definition from Wikipedia:

Copyright is a legal right, existing in many countries, that grants the creator of an original work exclusive rights to determine whether, and under what conditions, this original work may be used by others. This is usually only for a limited time.

If a person created a photograph after 1977, that person is said to own it, and all rights to that photograph, for their lifetime plus 70-years. If the picture was commissioned or published anonymously or under a pseudonym, the copyright would last for 95 years after publication or 120 years after creation, whichever is later.

You automatically own the copyright to any photograph you take. The problem may arise, if a photo of yours is stolen, proving that it is, in fact, your photograph. That's why it's wise to register your photographs with the copyright office in your country. Every country has a different procedure so it would be folly to try to list instructions here. Merely Google how to register a copyright for images, for your specific country.

If you do choose to register your copyright, you'll be eligible to sue for statutory damages up to, in the United States, $150,000. Otherwise, you'd only be able to sue for the expected fee earned if the image was sold plus, lawyer and filing fees.

The bottom line is that you own your pictures for your life and those rights will be transferred to your heirs after you die whether you register the copyright or don't.

Rights

Rights to your image are what you sell. You could sell a picture but only give the buyer the rights to use the image on their website. If they want to use it in an advertisement or on a billboard or even use it on their Instagram feed, that would be prohibited unless they purchase the individual rights for each of those uses.

The more ways they want to use the image, the more you should charge them for that image and never, ever, sell all rights to an image. What you're doing when you sell all rights, is giving up your copyright on that image. It is no longer yours because it's been purchased by your client. They own the photo and conceivably, they could not allow you to use the picture at all — not even in your portfolio. So, avoid selling all the rights to an image.

Whenever you negotiate a job, make sure it's obvious to your client what rights they get with your work — essentially, what they can and cannot do with YOUR pictures.

Part Two - Real Life Pricing Stories

For Part 2 of this guide, I asked two different photographers to share with us how they determine their pricing. Eric Jahn, explains all of the factors he considers when quoting prices for his wedding clients. Courtney Cutter describes how she takes advantage of a *Loss Leader*, photographing local bands, to gain more profitable work.

Wedding Photography Pricing and Consultation

By Eric Jahn

ericjahnphotography.com

As a wedding photographer there are many things you need to figure out and understand to create a smart and simple way to price out the cost for a potential client. Below I will explain what I have learned from much trial and error.

Upon receiving an inquiry form a potential, the first thing they express urgency on is what the final cost will be for services. These requests will come through via email or a social media direct message. This is a critical moment that could immediately scare off the potential client before even speaking with them. I try to avoid any sticker shock the potential client might feel when they receive a quote. The first thing I recommend is that you meet with the potential client in person for a consultation meeting to find out exactly what services you can provide and understand what price point will work for them.

Upon arriving to the consultation, I have found it to be extremely helpful to bring photographs and albums from previous weddings I have photographed to be used as a reference of my work. This gives the client a first hand impression of what type of work I have provided to my previous clients and they can assess if they like my style as well as the types of pictures they want to capture at their wedding. This helps drive much of the conversation and makes for a great tool to build the trust between myself and my potential client.

The first thing that has to be discussed about the upcoming wedding are the specific details. I have to know the specific dates/times, locations, and any other logistics of the day. This would include getting the names of all parties that will be in the wedding, groomsmen and bridesmaids. I also capture the names of any special family members that the couple wants to ensure are photographed with them on their wedding day. This could be parents, grandparents, siblings, and any other extended family members or very close friends. The more detail I can gather about the "who" is involved in the day, the less time I will spend searching for these people the day of the wedding. Once I have the detailed information above I like to understand what type or style of photography is the couple looking for, structured or candid shots. This is where the couple might spend more time looking at my previous weddings to decide of specific shots they really want to capture. Lastly the locations are important to discuss. Some couples like to visit many different locations to capture different looks and scenery. This is important to develop a detailed list of the day to ensure there is time to capture all the locations the couple wants to be photographed at. I find it very critical to understand how all of their wishes will fit into their busy day, the last thing the couple will want is to feel rushed and unorganized on their wedding day, and I take this as my responsibility as a professional photographer that wants to meet all their clients needs. Lastly, you have to discuss back up locations with the client due to the potential of inclement weather. No one wants to be stranded on their wedding day with no idea of where to take pictures in the event of a weather event that doesn't allow for planned outdoor photographs.

Finally to discuss pricing: Keep it simple. What does the couple want? One or two photographers, full day or half day services, wedding album and/or digital pictures? Once all of this is discussed you should be able to give an accurate and fair price for your services. The client will also have a greater understanding of the amount of work, time, and effort that goes into capturing a wedding.

There Isn't Any Money In Photographing Local bands. Why Do I Do It?

By Courtney Cutter

ccutterphoto.com

Photography is my passion, and it's fair to say that music is my second passion. I love to go to local venues to hear live music from my favorite artists and bands.

The natural thing is to combine my two passions and take pictures of the artists and photograph their shows. Unfortunately, there isn't money in it. The average musician can barely afford to put gas in their car to make it to their show so, charging profitable fees is not possible.

At best I'll get $40.00 to $50.00 to photograph their show, process the images, and put them on my website and Instagram. I may post up to 100 pictures that they can share on their social media, all they want. I do give them their choice of five, fully processed, full resolution, non-watermarked JPG's for use on print materials and show posters. They're instructed that they cannot use them for t-shirts or any other type of advertising, promotion or CD/Album covers without my consent.

For posed lifestyle images of the band or artist, I'll get $50.00 plus travel expenses, and again, I'll process the photos and put them on my website and social media for them to share. I'll give them five, fully processed, full resolution, non-watermarked JPG's for use on print materials and show posters with the same restrictions.

The key to for me to do this, for such little money, is advertising. I have a two-pronged approach:

1. When I'm photographing their show, I hand out business cards to anyone that talks to me. It's amazing how many people ask if I do a wedding, portrait, and/or senior photography. "Yes I do!" and I hand them my card.

2. When I put the musician's images online, I have them artfully watermarked so when they're shared, everyone who sees them will know who took them. I get a lot of referrals this way.

3. The artists win because they're getting professional images to share on their social media, plus a few photos to use on posters and print material, and I win because I get a ton of referrals for better-paying work such as weddings and senior pictures.

4. For me, I would have gone to those shows anyway. The little bit of money I do

make pays me for going, while at the same time, helping to get my brand noticed.

Part Three - 2019 Photography Pricing

In this part, I have the pricing listed for nineteen (19) different types of professional photography — from Band Photography to Wedding Photography.

At the end, I included a section called, *Add To Order* — The Add To Order section includes pricing for prints and photo products that can sold al a carte or added to any package prices listed in any of the nineteen different categories of pricing that are in this guide.

Band Photography

Band photography is popular but not very profitable. The term, Starving Musician is apropos. Usually, when a band is just starting out, playing small, local clubs, they won't have a lot of disposable income so you won't be able to charge them much. On the other hand, if they achieve a modicum of success, they'll have more money to spend. Unfortunately, that happens to very few bands, and if a group is lucky enough to become marginally successful, they'll usually have their photographer, in place. The key to being a successful band/music photographer is to work for peanuts with the bands that show promise. Ingratiate yourself to them early in their career, and if they catch a break, you'll most likely be taken along with them.

Band/Music photography is one of the types of photography where you should ask, "What is your budget?" because what bands can afford or be willing to pay will vary greatly, and it won't matter if they're a local club band or a national act. Once you know their budget, you can fit your pricing and services rendered so that you'll make a profit.

I did not break the pricing below down to *Beginner*, *Intermediate*, and *Expert* because the club playing band isn't interested in paying a premium for the expert photographer. They want images that they can share on social media and rarely will require any prints. So, the pricing is broken down by how successful the band is.

Local Club Band

$40.00 to photograph their local show

- Images on online gallery so they can share to social media

- Refer to the *Add To Order* pricing if they want prints or additional services beyond social media use

$75.00 to take posed images for their social media

- One hour session

- One wardrobe only. Add $20.00 for each additional wardrobe change

- Images on online gallery

- Refer to the *Add To Order* pricing if they want prints or additional services beyond social media use.

If a local "club band" wants to use one of the images you took for their indie CD cover, charge them $50.00

Regional Band playing venues over 1000 persons to 5000 persons

$200.00 to photograph their show beginning to end.
- Processed images on password protected online gallery
- Refer to the *Add To Order* pricing if they want any prints or additional services

$300 to take posed images for their social media
- One hour session
- One wardrobe only. Add $50.00 for each additional wardrobe change
- Images on online gallery
- Refer to the *Add To Order* pricing if they want prints or additional services

If a regional band wants to use one of the images you took for a CD cover, charge them $150.00

National band playing venues over 5000 persons

$1000.00 to photograph their show beginning to end
- Processed images on password protected online gallery
- Refer to the *Add To Order* pricing if they want any prints or additional services

$2500.00 to take posed images for their social media
- One hour session
- One wardrobe only. Add $200.00 for each additional wardrobe change
- Images on online gallery
- Refer to the *Add To Order* pricing if they want prints or additional services

If a national band wants to use one of the images you took for a CD cover, charge them $1500.00

If a national band requests that you take images for a magazine spread, this is usually paid for by the magazine so you should find out that magazine's budget and requirements for the shoot so you can price your work accordingly.

Birthing Sessions

Professional photographs of the birth of a child are becoming very popular. The main thing you must keep in mind if you want to pursue this type of photography is to know that you'll need to be on call, 24 hours a day, 7 days a week, for approximately one month before your client's due date and possibly, a couple of weeks after their due date because, quite naturally, birthing sessions take place whenever your client gives birth to her child.

Because of this, birthing sessions are usually charged at a premium. The pricing below is meant as a starting point for the standard package listed. Please refer to the *Add To Order* section for any additional product or services.

Before you book a birthing session, make sure that the hospital and doctor allow it. You can check the hospitals in your area to see if photography is approved and you should ask your client to get written approval from their doctor. Some hospitals and doctors will have no restrictions, but most will only allow you in the birthing suite after the baby is born. It's essential that both you and your client know when and where you're allowed to shoot before you show up at the hospital.

Package

Beginner $500.00 - Intermediate $700.00 - Expert $1000.00

Pre-consultation

4-6 weeks on call

Hospital coverage during birth and one hour after birth.

Hospital coverage for one hour the day-after the birth (Photographs of baby with relatives).

4 - 8x10

4 - 5x7

16 - wallets

Shareable Online gallery (Gallery of watermarked images that is of high enough resolution to share on social media but not high enough to print)

Refer to the *Add To Order* section for additional products

Alternate Package

Often photographers prefer to offer a Print Credit instead of supplying a specific number and sizes of packaged prints. When doing this, they have non-watermarked images on the online gallery and have them online at full resolution. The customer will use the print credit to have you (or your lab), print some of the images but have the option of downloading the pictures and printing them, themselves. That is why this package costs slightly more.

Beginner $600.00 - Intermediate $800.00 - Expert $1100.00

Each include a $150.00 Print Credit

Pre-consultation

4-6 weeks on call

Hospital coverage during birth and one hour after birth.

Hospital coverage for one hour the day-after the birth (Photographs of baby with relatives).

Shareable, downloadable, online gallery.

Refer to the *Add To Order* section for additional products

Boudoir

Boudoir portraiture has been very popular for many years, and it seems to be sustaining its popularity. Boudoir portraiture is intimate images of a person — usually but not always, a woman. I've seen Boudoir done for men and couples as well, so keep an open mind! Nude photography is not considered Boudoir.

Prices shown below do not include hair and makeup. You can advise your client to arrive with their hair and makeup done but, usually, boudoir photography includes the services of a hair and makeup artist. If you're serious about doing boudoir photography, you should hire the services of a hair/makeup artist and add their cost to the prices shown below. You should mark up the amount they're charging you between 15% and 100%. So, if your makeup person is charging you $100.00 to do your client's hair and makeup, you should bill your client between $115.00 and $200.00 for the service. Add that amount to the package price below.

The pricing below is meant as a starting point. Please refer to the *Add To Order* section for any additional product or services.

I broke the pricing down for three different types of photographers — *Beginner*, *Intermediate*, and *Expert*.

Package

Beginner $175.00 - Intermediate $250.00 - Expert $350.00
1-2 hour session including 2 outfit changes
2 - 8x10
4 - 5x7
Password-Protected Online Gallery of watermarked images
Refer to the *Add To Order* section for additional products.

Alternate Package

Often photographers prefer to offer a Print Credit instead of supplying a specific number and sizes of packaged prints. When doing this, they have non-watermarked images on the online gallery and have them online at full resolution. The customer will use the print credit to have you (or your lab), print some of the images but have the option of downloading the pictures and printing them, themselves. That is why these packages cost slightly more.

Beginner $225.00 - Intermediate $300.00 - Expert $400.00

Each include a $50.00 Print Credit

1-2 hour session including 2 outfit changes

Password-Protected Online Gallery

Refer to the *Add To Order* section for additional products.

Concert Photography

Concert Photography is quite popular, but it's typically not a money-making endeavor. Most concert photographers do it for the love of music.

Concert photos are used in magazines, websites, and blogs, but the pay isn't substantial for the vast majority of the photographers that do this type of work. Partly, this is because of the limitations imposed upon the photographer by the artist.

To shoot a concert, you must get a photographer's pass from either the venue, the promoter, or, most commonly, through the band/performer's management. Typically this is secured via email 2-3 weeks before the show, and the performer will want to know what you're shooting them for — they usually will only want to give out a photo pass to a photographer that can help promote them. So, if you're shooting for a national music magazine or a popular music blog, you'll have a better chance of securing the pass than if you're shooting for your portfolio. So, if you want to shoot concerts, it would be in your best interest to contact a blog or magazine that you think could be interested in the photos of that artist and ask them, ahead of time, if you can use them as a reference to get the photo pass.

Finally, most artists will ask you to sign a contract. Some artists have a contract that is quite demanding stating that all of the pictures you take, are the property of the performer and you cannot sell them. Other artists are a bit more lenient.

When you do secure your photo pass and show up to take the pictures, you'll be funneled to the photographer's pit which is a spot directly in front of the stage allowing you to capture unobstructed views of the performer(s). Unfortunately, you'll be allowed to take pictures for, at most, the first three songs then, you'll be escorted out -- this will vary from band to band, performer to performer. Some will only allow photographers for the first song while others may allow for three. Either way, you'll need to shoot quickly and include everything you need to cover.

Once you have the pictures you'll have to abide by the contract but, assuming that you're able to sell them, you have a few limited opportunities:

Local Newspapers
The local newspaper may be interested in one of your photos for their entertainment section. You can expect to be paid between $25.00 and $40.00 for this photo.

Regional Blogs & Websites
This is likely where the majority of your images can be seen. Unfortunately, you'll notice

I wrote *seen* and not *sold*. Regional blogs and websites usually will not have a budget for pictures and will instead offer you a photographer's byline and a link to your portfolio or website.

National Blogs & Websites

It's difficult, but you might be able to sell an image or two to a popular music oriented, national blog or national website. Also, these are the places you should email when you're seeking references to secure your photo pass. Letting them know ahead of time that you're shooting a specific show not only allows you to pre-gauge their interest, it then will give you the in to send them your images on spec. When they purchase photos on spec, it, unfortunately, isn't for much — expect to get $25.00 to $50.00 for single images and $200.00 for a cover. If you can ingratiate yourself to them by shooting and selling on spec, you might be able to get an assignment. Assignments from National Blogs & Websites pay $350.00 to $500.00 per day plus expenses.

National Magazines

Almost impossible. National magazines such as Rolling Stone Magazine have a stable of photographers they use. Either directly employed by them or others they hire for features. To shoot music and concert photography for a National Magazine will require you to build your portfolio and get hired by them on the strength of your work.

Corporate Photography

Many professionals such as doctors, lawyers, engineers and the like, require headshots for their website, publication, and ads. Headshot photography can be very profitable, and many photographers specialize in this type of shooting.

Often, a company may require photographs for their annual report or corporate newsletter — for that type of photography, refer to the section on Event Photography.

There are two packages listed below — digital only and digital with prints. Often, the company will require a picture of the employee to be hung in a common area such as the front office, waiting room, or an entrance hallway.

If you're taking pictures of more than five (5) individuals, from a company, at one time, you can discount the pricing shown between 10% - 25%

Package One - Digital Only (per person)

Beginner $50.00 — Intermediate $85.00 — Expert $150.00

One Outfit — Add 50% for each additional outfit

15 minutes shooting per subject

Professional retouching

3-5 digital images of each outfit, large enough for websites, publications, and online/print ads

Package Two - Digital Plus Prints (per person)

Beginner $100.00 — Intermediate $145.00 — Expert $250.00

One Outfit — Add 25% for each additional outfit

15 minutes shooting per subject

Professional retouching

3-5 digital images of each outfit, large enough for websites, publications, and online/print ads

(2) 8x10

(2) 5x7

(16) wallets

Engagement Sessions

Often, engagement photos are included in the packages and pricing of the wedding photos — this pricing is intended for when they aren't.

Like wedding photography, prices for engagement sessions vary widely. If you're a total beginner or an intermediate photographer, the pricing below will work out well. On the other hand, if you're an expert photographer with an extensive portfolio and you're relatively well known, you'll almost be able to name your price, so the Expert prices shown below are averages.

Typically, engagements are charged on an hourly rate with the images being supplied on a shareable website. I recommend that you watermark the photos so when they are shared, you'll get some free advertising.

Prints are purchased at the *Add To Order* pricing, and I suggest that all packages include a print credit.

Package #1

Beginner - $150.00 Intermediate - $225.00 Expert - $400.00

One hour shoot

One wardrobe

72-hour turnaround

30 - 50 processed images posted to shareable online gallery for 90-days

$50.00 print credit

Package #2

Beginner - $250.00 Intermediate - $425.00 Expert - $650.00

One to two hour shoot

Two wardrobes

72-hour turnaround

50 - 100 processed images posted to shareable online gallery for 90-days

$100.00 print credit

Package #3

Beginner - $350.00 Intermediate - $525.00 Expert - $800.00

One to three hour shoot

Three wardrobes

72-hour turnaround

75 - 150 processed images posted to shareable online gallery for 90-days

20 fully processed digital images

$100.00 print credit

Add-Ons

24-hour turnaround - $100.00

Downloadable online gallery for 180-days - $100.00 (Make sure this is priced taking into account any fees you're being charged to have the images online.)

Travel more than 25-miles - $100.00 per hour of travel time

Event Photography

Event Photography most often refers to corporate parties and meetings but also could include large family reunions, sports banquets, and ethnic festivals. Any gathering of people that isn't done often can be considered an event.

Often event photography is photojournalistic in nature, but you'll often have to shoot posed groups as well. Proper lighting will be required. Make sure you know ahead of time what the venue looks like and what you're expected to shoot so you'll then know if you need to bring strobes, an assistant, or if you, your camera, and flash will suffice.

Pricing for event photography is per hour, and usually, prints are not supplied but instead, a downloadable online gallery is provided. Prints can be sold at the *Add To Order* pricing.

Rights are an essential facet of event photography, and they should be made clear. Most often the photographer retains ownership of the images but does allow the photos to be used, by the person or organization that booked the event, for *Commercial Use* - this means that they can use the images in just about any way they'd like as long as they don't claim ownership of the pictures. The photographer is the owner and retains the right to sell them as well.

Some organizations may want ownership of the images — it is strongly recommended that a photographer not, under any circumstances, give up ownership of their images but if you must, triple all of the event pricing shown.

In researching Event Photography, I found that there isn't a lot of disparity, so I only have two photographer groups listed — Inexperienced and Experienced. If you don't have an event portfolio built up, you're inexperienced.

You can offer one package — with an hourly fee and charge more for add-ons as listed.

Finally, make sure you have it clear with the event organizers that you're shooting for a precise length of time. For example, make it clear that you'll be shooting their event for say, 2.5 hours and you expect to be paid for 2.5 hours. Too often you'll encounter that if you don't let them know this up front, after the fact, they'll hedge at paying you the amount of time you spent shooting. Also, get a substantial deposit before the event the balance due, the day of the event.

Standard Package
Inexperienced - $150.00 per hour Experienced - $300.00 per hour
50-100 images taken per hour

72-hour turnaround

Processed images posted to downloadable online gallery for 90-days

Commercial Rights

Add-Ons

24-hour turnaround - Add $100.00

Downloadable online gallery for 180-days - Add $100.00 (Make sure this is priced taking into account any fees you're being charged to have the images online.)

Travel more than 25-miles - Add $100.00 per hour of travel time

Assistant for large events or events requiring gear other than camera and flash - Double what you're paying your assistant. So, if you're paying your assistant $50.00 per hour, charge the event organizers $100.00 per hour for your assistant.

Fine Art

There is a fine line between offering prints of your pictures and offering *Fine Art Prints* of your images. Although there is a tremendous difference between a drugstore print and a print that was created by the photographer or a quality print lab, made on archival paper and inks, what is considered to be *Fine Art* is open for interpretation. For the sake of this discussion and pricing, I consider a fine art print to be one that is created at a minimum, on high-quality archival paper using high-quality archival ink. It can be printed by the photographer or by a professional print lab.

To determine the pricing shown below, I surveyed the top professional photo labs in the world to come up with an average print cost. I then studied the market to see what others were offering and charging, and from there, I determined the pricing you should charge for your prints. If you print yourself, you'll not only have more control over the final product, but you'll enjoy a more significant profit margin.

While looking at the market, I noticed a tremendous difference in pricing between photographers. I found relative new photographers offering substandard work at high prices and at the same time, I found somewhat established photographers offering their work at a substantial discount. I'm reasonably certain the unknown photographer with high rates isn't selling too many prints while I'm equally sure that the reasonably well-known photographer, selling at a discount, is leaving a substantial amount of money on the table. So, the pricing I came up is in three different categories — *Unknown*, *Well Known*, and *Very Well Known*. The pricing is set so that if you have quality work and if nobody has ever heard of you, you'll be able to sell prints in the current market. At the same time, if you're a bit more well known, you won't have to be concerned about leaving any money on the table.

Making a living as a fine art photographer is nearly impossible unless you're relatively well known. With that said, many photographers can supplement their income by offering fine art prints although, as you'll see below, the pricing can vary significantly from the unknown photographer through to the very well known photographer and to be quite honest, the very well known photographer can usually name their price, and they'll get it.

Many photographers offer discounts on multiple prints. Usually, they're not offering a percentage discount but instead offering a free or reduced-priced print when a certain number are purchased. For example, an unknown photographer may be offering 8x10 prints for $15.00 each, but if their customer buys two (2), they'll get the third at 1/2 price. So, they'd get the three (3) 8x10 prints for $37.50.

If you choose to offer discounts, It doesn't matter how you set it up, remember you're giving your customer incentive to get at least one more print for a drastically reduced price as long as that drastically reduced price still returns a profit.

One mistake many beginners make is that they offer too many sizes. You'll find that if a person likes one of your images, they'll buy a size that fits their budget. Offering too many sizes can cause confusion and hesitation and hesitation may cost you a sale — I show more sizes than you'll need to inventory — sell the sizes that make the most sense for you.

Shipping from the lab to you and shipping from you to your customer should be added to the prices shown below.

Pricing If You're Unknown

Giclée Prints

Giclée Prints prints are created on the highest quality paper with archival ink and usually have a glossy or satin finish.

8x10	$30.00
11x14	$40.00
16x24	$70.00
20x30	$100.00
24x36	$130.00

Canvas Gallery Wraps

Quality Canvas wrapped around a 1.5" wood frame.

8x10	$70.00
11x14	$85.00
16x24	$130.00
20x30	$170.00
24x36	$230.00

Metal Prints

Prints on aluminum with standard mounting posts.

(The price to manufacture a metal print goes up substantially as the print gets larger)

8x10	$35.00
11x14	$60.00
16x24	$115.00
20x30	$160.00
24x36	$275.00

Acrylic Prints

Lustre Prints with a 1/4" acrylic surface and standard mounting posts.

Many famous Fine Art photographers offer their work in Acrylic only.

Because of the price point, it may be difficult for a unknown photographer to sell acrylic prints.

8x10	$85.00
11x14	$120.00
16x24	$180.00
20x30	$230.00
24x36	$315.00

Pricing If You're Well Known

Giclée Prints

Giclée Prints prints are created on the highest quality paper with archival ink and usually have a glossy or satin finish.

8x10	$40.00
11x14	$50.00
16x24	$90.00
20x30	$135.00
24x36	$170.00

Canvas Gallery Wraps

Quality Canvas wrapped around a 1.5" wood frame.

8x10	$90.00
11x14	$110.00
16x24	$170.00
20x30	$220.00
24x36	$295.00

Metal Prints

Prints on aluminum with standard mounting posts.

(The price to manufacture a metal print goes up substantially as the print gets larger)

8x10	$40.00
11x14	$75.00
16x24	$150.00
20x30	$200.00
24x36	$350.00

Acrylic Prints

Lustre Prints with a 1/4" acrylic surface and standard mounting posts.

Many famous Fine Art photographers offer their work in Acrylic only.

8x10	$110.00
11x14	$155.00
16x24	$230.00
20x30	$295.00
24x36	$400.00

Pricing If You're Very Well Known

Giclée Prints

Giclée Prints prints are created on the highest quality paper with archival ink and usually have a glossy or satin finish.

8x10	$75.00
11x14	$100.00
16x24	$150.00
20x30	$225.00
24x36	$275.00

Canvas Gallery Wraps

Quality Canvas wrapped around a 1.5" wood frame.

8x10	$130.00
11x14	$175.00
16x24	$250.00
20x30	$350.00
24x36	$460.00

Metal Prints

Prints on aluminum with standard mounting posts.

(The price to manufacture a metal print goes up substantially as the print gets larger)

8x10	$65.00
11x14	$125.00
16x24	$230.00
20x30	$310.00
24x36	$500.00

Acrylic Prints

Lustre Prints with a 1/4" acrylic surface and standard mounting posts. Many famous Fine Art photographers offer their work in Acrylic only.

8x10	$150.00
11x14	$200.00
16x24	$300.00
20x30	$360.00
24x36	$550.00

General Portraiture

General portraiture involves photographing a person, persons, family, or group in the studio or, in what is often called, Lifestyle Photography — that is, shooting them at their home or outside. Outside could be anywhere from their yard to a national park.

General portraiture encompasses several different types of photography, including and not limited to: family — holiday or yearly family photos, children, all sorts of anniversaries, engagement, maternity, baby gender reveal, etc.

If you're traveling to them — that is, traveling some distance, in your vehicle for the shoot, you need to make sure you account for the gas, tolls, and wear and tear on your car so make sure you add any traveling related costs to the package prices shown below.

You should offer no more than three (3) packages, as listed below and you should collect a *Sitting Fee* when you book the shoot. The sitting fee is INCLUDED in the prices shown below. The sitting fee is usually 10% to 50% of the total package price. So, a package that runs $150.00 includes a sitting fee of between $15.00 and $75.00.

One thing you can add to any of the packages, although I recommend adding it to package 3, is a Print Credit for a specific amount. For example, a beginner can take Package 3 that runs, $75.00 but add a $50.00 print credit to the price. So, the beginner would offer that package, as it's listed below, but add a $50.00 print credit to the package and advertise it for $125.00. The prints are sold at the *Add To Order* prices as listed in this guide.

I divided the pricing into three photographer groups: *Beginner*, *Intermediate*, and *Expert*.

Package 1

Beginner - $150.00 Intermediate - $200.00 Expert - $300.00

Two (2) outfit changes

1-2 hours of picture taking

Sharable online gallery with watermarked images of high enough resolution for social media sharing

2 - 8x10 prints

4 - 5x7 prints

16 - wallets

20 - fully processed, full resolution, JPG images on thumb drive

Refer to the To-Order section for additional products

Package 2

Beginner - $100.00 Intermediate - $150.00 Expert - $250.00

Two (2) outfit changes

1-2 hours of picture taking

Sharable online gallery with watermarked images of high enough resolution for social media sharing

1 - 8x10 print

2 - 5x7 prints

15 - fully processed, full resolution, JPG images on thumb drive

Refer to the To-Order section for additional products

Package 3

Beginner - $75.00 Intermediate - $100.00 Expert - $200.00

Two (2) outfit changes

1-2 hours of picture taking

Sharable online gallery with watermarked images of high enough resolution for social media sharing

15 - fully processed, full resolution, JPG images on thumb drive

Refer to the To-Order section for additional products and consider using this package if you want to add a print credit

Magazine Photography

Types of Magazines

There are four different types of magazines. All of them buy pictures and employ freelance photographers so don't just pursue the consumer magazine market — there are hundreds of different magazines on the market although you'll find that some don't pay very well and others are hard to break in to.

Consumer Magazines are aimed at the general public and are what you'll often see on the magazine rack at the grocery store. *Family Circle*, *Sports Illustrated*, and *Men's Health* are examples of Consumer Magazines.

Trade Magazines are aimed at people with specific occupations or trades. *U.S. Banker*, *Restaurant*, and *PrintWeek* are examples of Trade Magazines.

Corporate Magazines are magazines produced by major corporations targeted to their customers. The goal of these magazines isn't to necessarily generate a profit but to promote their brand. *Rhapsody* (United Airlines), *Pineapple* (Airbnb), and *The Red Bulletin* (Red Bull) are examples of Corporate Magazines.

Association Magazines are aimed at large member groups. *Sierra Magazine* (Sierra Club), *The Humanist* (American Humanist Association), and *Diabetes Forecast* (The American Diabetes Association) are examples of Association Magazines.

Pricing

Most often, established magazine photographers receive an assignment from a magazine with an agreed upon payment, per-day, plus expenses. Other times, a photographer may have the photographs and story done and will approach the magazine with it — in those cases, the magazine, if interested, will pay a per-page amount. Other times, magazines need to purchase a picture or two to compliment a feature or as standalone photographs.

Local Magazines - Unfortunately, local magazines have a surplus of local, amateur photographers, willing to work for free just to see their name in print. Equally unfortunately, if you want to break into taking photographs for magazines, you'll need to start at the local level. You'll find that you'll need to work for free to build up your portfolio and resume. At best you'll be able to get your expenses reimbursed and be paid a small amount for a cover photo — $25.00 - $50.00.

Trade, Corporate, and Association Magazines - Pay on average $100.00 to

$500.00 per day plus expenses for assignments. For freelance features, they'll pay between $100.00 to $500.00 per page. Individual photographs are most often purchased from stock photo sites, but if they find that you have something intriguing, they'll buy it for between $50.00 and $150.00.

Regional Magazines, and Smaller National Magazines - Pay $250.00 to $750.00 per day plus expenses for assignments. For freelance features, they'll pay $500.00 to $1000.00 per page. Pay will vary significantly for individual photographs — from $25.00 to $250.00.

Major Publications - major publications such as National Geographic and People Magazine often have five to six-figure budgets for feature shoots. You'll find that they most often have a stable of photographers that they work with. Your best chance to get in with them is to make friends with all the publishers, art directors, editors, and designers along the way. People are continually moving in jobs and the editor of the regional magazine you worked with today could become an associate editor at a major publication tomorrow and still have you in their contact list. Stay in touch and accessible and, as long as your work is good and you're reliable, you'll eventually catch a break.

Mini Sessions

Mini Sessions are becoming quite popular. They're merely a very short photographic session. — always less than a 1/2 hour in length with the delivery, via email or Dropbox, of a number of fully processed JPG's.

There could be numerous reasons why a person may need a mini-session. It could be that they need a picture for their blog or perhaps a photo for a book they've written. Often, because of the person's limited need, they won't want to commit to a full photo session with wardrobe changes. They want you to take several pictures and give them a few to choose from.

The number of JPG's supplied determines the pricing, and I broke the pricing down between *Beginner*, *Intermediate*, and *Expert*.

Any additional product should be charged at the *Add To Order* pricing.

Package 1
Beginner $50.00 - Intermediate $100.00 - Expert $150.00
Electronic delivery of up to ten (10) fully processed, JPG images.

Package 2
Beginner $75.00 - Intermediate $150.00 - Expert $225.00
Electronic delivery of up to twenty (20) fully processed, JPG images.

Newborns

Newborn photography is trendy and very profitable but, you need to have an immense amount of patience to photograph newborn babies. Also, you'll need to have, on hand, creative props. These are usually cute beds that the infant will be sleeping in while you photograph them. I've seen these beds made to resemble sunflowers — with a matching sunflower hat for the baby, race cars, centipedes, and kittens. A quick online search will give you a ton of ideas — all you'll need is the ability to build the bed and of course, make sure that it's safe and sanitary.

Most newborn photographers supply a specific number of fully processed JPG images, and some also offer a print credit.

I divided the pricing into three photographer groups: *Beginner, Intermediate, and Expert.*

Package #1

Beginner $300.00 - Intermediate $500.00 - Expert $800.00

2 - 2.5 hr session

Includes family pose with baby

1 prop setup

Use of props and accessories provided by photographer

Shareable Online gallery (Gallery of watermarked images that is of high enough resolution to share on social media but not high enough to print)

20 fully edited high resolution images on thumb drive or made available via digital download

Prints can be purchased from the online gallery at the *Add To Order* pricing

Package #2

Beginner $400.00 - Intermediate $600.00 - Expert $900.00

Includes family pose with baby

Includes parent pose with baby

Includes sibling pose with baby

2 prop setups

Use of props and accessories provided by photographer

Shareable Online gallery (Gallery of watermarked images that is of high enough resolution to share on social media but not high enough to print)

30 fully edited high resolution images on thumb drive or made available via digital

download

Prints can be purchased from the online gallery at the *Add To Order* pricing.

Photojournalism

In its purest form, a Photojournalist tells stories with pictures — most often of news events or stories with a newsworthy subject matter. Photojournalists are often fully employed by newspapers, news magazines, and news organizations, but often, they'll need to hire freelancers or stringers outside of their employ.

Who Hires Photojournalists?

National Daily Newspapers

The New York Times, USA Today, Washington Post, Metro US, The Guardian London, and the *Los Angeles Times* often employ freelance photographers to fill a need — often that need is for work outside of the paper's geographical area. For example, if there is a story in Paris that needs to be covered, the *Los Angeles Times*, instead of enduring the cost of sending one of their photographers to France, will hire a local Parisian photojournalist to cover the story.

Wire Services

Wire services distribute news content to media outlets such as newspapers, magazines, news websites, etc. Those places subscribe to the wire service and can use the material as it's delivered. The top players in this field are the Associated Press and Reuters.

Local Newspapers

Most local newspapers hire local photojournalists to help cover local news, sports, and spot news — that is coverage of a spontaneous news event such as a massive fire or plane crash.

Some local papers have an agreement with their photographer's union that they will not hire any local freelancers or stringers for local stories except for spot news coverage although they do have the freedom to hire photojournalists for news outside of the area. For example, I was contacted by a local Australian newspaper to cover Donald Trump when he, while campaigning for president, was coming through my hometown of Buffalo, New York.

Magazines

Time Magazine is the only major news magazine left in the United States that regularly hires freelance photojournalists. It is my understanding that *U.S. News & World Report* only hires for spot news.

Niche Newspapers

Most major cities have niche newspapers that cover a narrow topic. Usually, they don't pay very well (or at all), but they're an excellent place to start your career in photojournalism and where you should work to build your resume.

Online Publications

Slate, Salon, Yahoo, Buzzfeed, Huffington Post, and dozens of others are examples of online publications although, unfortunately, they rarely hire photojournalists opting to use wire services instead.

Fees

The fee one can get from any of the potential buyers listed above is dependent on the size of the organization. Assignment fees can range from $50.00 per day from the local Niche Newspapers to $500.00, plus expenses, from the National Daly Newspapers.

Some clients prefer to pay a day rate and may ask you what your day rate is -- this is a tricky way of them to get you to do work at a lower price because, what constitutes a day, is up for debate and whether or not expenses are covered often will get lost in the shuffle. If a client asks you what your day rate is, ask them what their budget is. Say that maybe you'll be able to adjust your day rate to fit their budget.

Another thing that has an impact on fees are usage rights. The more rights they want, the more you should charge for your work. Again, you'll have to ask them what their budget is and negotiate the rights you'll sell within the constraints of their budget.

If your client is trying to hire you using the term, 'Work Made For Hire,' that means that they retain all of the rights to the images and you'll have none — you probably won't even be allowed to use the pictures in your portfolio. You should never do 'Work Made For Hire' unless they're paying you a five-figure fee.

Bottom Line

You're not going to make substantial money unless a national newspaper or wire service hire you. Anything less than that, aim to get $50.00 to $200.00 per assignment, plus expenses. Try not to get trapped into a day rate.

If you do get an assignment by a national newspaper or wire service, pricing will depend on how involved, travel intensive, and dangerous the assignment is so, the pricing will vary greatly. They likely will say, this is what we want you to do and this is what we pay. If you're new and can afford to take their initial offer, then do. Once you prove to them the quality of your work, you can, from that point forward, negotiate a higher fee.

If you're interested in Photojournalism, I suggest you join the National Press Photographers Association (NPPA). There you'll find more advice on how to get and price your work.

https://www.nppa.org/

Prom Photography

Prom photography is relatively easy and can be quite profitable. The profit per couple isn't very high, but almost every couple that goes to their prom will get professional pictures taken so you'll have a willing, captive audience. Additionally, you'll be paid fully, in advance for your work. So what prom photography lacks in profit margin, it makes up for in volume and immediate payment.

One dark side of prom photography is that often, the photographer, to secure the gig, will have to donate something toward the prom. Most often, it's a monetary donation to go toward the ticket printing or a gift of the prom favors that each couple will receive at their table. In the industry, it's not considered ethical to give a kickback to secure a contract so try to avoid doing this. Also, in some states and localities, it may be illegal.

Like, school and sports team photography, you'll have to supply the envelopes, poly bags and all of the pricing info for your customer to fill out and give to you at picture time.

Most venues that are geared toward proms will have an area or and attractive *set* for the prom pictures -- this will often be a flowered arch or a small gazebo. Check the venue before the prom to see where the photos will be taken. If the site does not have a set, you'll have to bring backgrounds. Bring several different backgrounds so you can choose the background that will best complement the clothing of the subjects. You'll have to have backgrounds that can be easily and quickly switched out.

You're going to need two lights with a simple light setup consisting of the fill light by the camera and the key light at a 45-degree angle from the camera.

You'll be taking pictures of a single pose. I suggest you have a poster that illustrates several different available poses for the couple and have them choose the pose that works for them.

Since prom photography doesn't have a large, per package, profit, I only broke the pricing down into two categories — *Beginner* and *Expert*.

Package A

Beginner - $69.00 Expert - $89.00

4 - 8x10

6 - 5x7

6 - 4x6

32 - wallets

Package B

Beginner - $59.00 Expert - $79.00

3 - 8x10

4 - 5x7

5 - 4x6

24 - wallets

Package C

Beginner - $49.00 Expert - $69.00

2 - 8x10

2 - 5x7

4 - 4x6

16 - wallets

Package D

Beginner - $29.00 Expert - $49.00

2 - 8x10

8 - wallets

Add-On

At times, a prom couple may want one of the prom packages above, but they'd also like solo shots of either one of them or both of them. If that is the case, have them pick a second package for each additional pose but reduce the price of that package by 10% to 25%.

For example, a couple may have purchased package "B" at the Expert Price of $69.00 but, the young lady's parents would like a picture of their daughter, alone. They can add package "D" for that picture and save 10% to 25% off the price of package "D" because it was purchased along with package "B".

School Pictures

Most school pictures are done by large, photography businesses that specialize in this type of work. You'll find that they most often will have the market cornered from kindergarten through 11th grade having signed multi-year contracts with the larger school districts. You'll have better luck doing this type of photography for private and parochial schools. Senior pictures are another matter, and I have a separate category and pricing for them.

Price points won't matter if you're a beginner, intermediate, or expert. You have to supply the service and produce the work on time. You will be able to charge a bit more if you are photographing private schools and some parochial schools, so I've broken down the pricing into two categories — *Public School* and *Private School*.

The emphasis is on delivering prints, so all packages are print packages. Note that you'll have to supply all the material to the parents that describe all of the packages with clear instructions on how to fill out the forms and make full, pre-payment. So, the good news is that you'll be paid fully before you do anything. Also, note that most public schools or public school districts will insist on one reasonably priced package meaning, they'll ask that you offer one package for less than $20.00.

Finally, you should have an option to fix acne in post-production -- parents often request this. So, on the forms, you give to the parents describing the packages, include an *air brush* option for acne and charge $25.00 to $50.00 for the service. If you're doing the photographs for a higher priced private school, you can charge $50.00 to $100.00.

Public School

Package A, $69.00

4 - 8x10

6 - 5x7

6 - 4x6

32 - wallets

Package B, $59.00

3 - 8x10

4 - 5x7

5 - 4x6

24 - wallets

Package C, $49.00

2 - 8x10

2 - 5x7

4 - 4x6

16 - wallets

Package D, $19.00

1 - 8x10

8 - wallets

Private School

Package A, $89.00

4 - 8x10

6 - 5x7

6 - 4x6

32 - wallets

Package B, $79.00

3 - 8x10

4 - 5x7

5 - 4x6

24 - wallets

Package C, $69.00

2 - 8x10

2 - 5x7

4 - 4x6

16 - wallets

Package D, $39.00

1 - 8x10

8 - wallets

Seniors

In my research, I've found the most pricing discrepancy in Senior Portraiture. There are a lot of photographers doing it and the prices, and services offered, vary greatly.

Some photographers offer digital only while others provide print and digital options. My pricing below is broken down into two categories, *Digital Only* packages and *Prints, and Digital* packages. If you choose *Digital Only*, you can sell prints at the *Add To Order* pricing. Likewise, if you're offering *Prints and Digital*, you can sell additional prints at the *Add To Order* pricing.

Finally, I've broken the pricing down to two photographer groups — *Inexperienced* and *Experienced*. This type of photography is too competitive to break it down any further. For this type of photography, I suggest you research your market — you'll find that packages and prices will widely vary and if your market is saturated and you're an experienced photographer, you may have to price your services at the inexperienced level.

Digital Only

Package #1
Inexperienced - $75.00 Experienced - $125.00
20-minute session
1 wardrobe
Traditional yearbook poses
No Props
Up to 20 images on online gallery
(Meant for the family that does not have the budget for more expensive, more common senior packages)

Package #2
Inexperienced - $125.00 Experienced - $200.00
60-minute session
2 wardrobes
1 prop
Traditional and casual yearbook poses
Up to 40 images on online gallery

Package #3
Inexperienced - $200.00 Experienced - $300.00
90-minute session
3-4 wardrobes
2 props
Traditional and casual yearbook poses
Up to 80 images on online gallery

Digital and Print

Package #1
Inexperienced - $125.00 Experienced - $175.00
20-minute session
1 wardrobe
Traditional yearbook poses
No Props
Up to 20 images on online gallery
1 - 8x10
16 - wallets
(Meant for the family that does not have the budget for more expensive, more common senior packages)

Package #2
Inexperienced - $200.00 Experienced - $275.00
60-minute session
2 wardrobes
1 prop
Traditional and casual yearbook poses
Up to 40 images on online gallery
2 - 8x10
4 - 5x7
16 - wallets

Package #3

Inexperienced - $300.00 Experienced - $400.00

90-minute session

3-4 wardrobes

2 props

Traditional and casual yearbook poses

Up to 80 images on online gallery

4 - 8x10

4 - 5x7

32 - wallets

Social Media Photography

Social Media Photography is relatively new. The popularity of applications such as Instagram and SnapChat have fostered a new kind of model — a model that garners large followings by merely posting pictures of themselves, on social media, doing interesting things. They even have a term for these people: *Influencers*. Once the Influencer has grown their following, they begin to get paid by companies to use that company's product in their posts. For example, a woman with a huge Instagram following — I'm talking about a person with an audience of over several million, will be paid to wear a specific designer's jeans or earrings and have those pictures posted to their Instagram and other social media accounts.

Often, the models will need their social media images done professionally -- this can be the up-and-coming model who doesn't have a significant following yet, but wants professional photos to help them gain that following, or the established model that is already being followed by millions. Both often need the services of a professional photographer, but your pricing should be different between the two. You need to charge substantially more for the images that are going to be seen by more people and less for those that are just beginning their career. This is similar to band photography in that the beginning model, like the local club band, likely won't be able to afford to pay you much and the established model, like the world-renowned band, can afford to pay more but probably already has his or her photographer in place. Your best opportunity to break into Social Media Photography is to work for peanuts with the up-and-coming models and hope they hit it big and take you along for the ride.

Images are almost always digital. If a rare print is needed, it can be priced at the *Add To Order* Pricing.

Pricing is broken down by the number of followers the model has.

0 to 1-Million Followers

Although 1-million may seem like a lot of followers, it isn't enough where the model will be getting a plethora of lucrative offers so you won't be able to charge too much and your experience won't matter. $25.00 to $50.00 per image or, if you're doing a shoot, $100.00 per hour. Images are supplied digitally through email or an online service such as DropBox or Google Drive.

Over 1-Million Followers

Now the model is likely getting substantial offers -- this is the situation where you must ask them what their budget is and what the photo requirements are. The reason is that the offers and requirements they get will vary greatly. They might be offered $1000.00 to wear a specific pair of earrings from company "A", and need to post two pictures of those earrings yet in another situation, be offered $10,000.00 to wear a bikini by company "B" that requires ten posted images. You're working harder for "B", the model is earning more for "B", so you should charge more for "B".

Chances are if they want you to do their pictures, they like something about your photography, and your style that they think will benefit them so don't be afraid to negotiate your fee because they'll likely low-ball their budget to you. Just be clear what is expected, by them, from you, so you can best price the job.

Sports Teams

In most aspects, sport team photography is similar to school picture photography. Your customer will choose, before the shoot, from a number of print packages that are printed on paperwork and envelopes that you supply. You'll be prepaid and will, in a timely fashion, need to supply the finished product to the customer.

Usually this type of photography is for team sports such as baseball, football, soccer and so on and it will consist of you taking one picture of each of the players and one group photo of all the players and coaches. All of the packages will include the group photo and vary as far as the size and quantity of the individual image.

Only one individual pose is taken and it will usually be done on location. In the case of outdoor sports, you would schedule a picture day along with an alternate rain day. Typically the individual photos are taken without any backdrop instead using the field as the natural backdrop. You can bring a portable strobe with softbox to light the subject or use a reflector. Try to locate your subjects in the shade and be wary of dappled light. Make sure the existing light is even on their face and body. In the case of indoor sports like basketball and hockey, you'll need to use a strobe or off camera flash.

You'll pose the individual in uniform and sometimes with a prop — for example, baseball players will hold a baseball bat in a batting stance or a basketball player will have a ball under their arm.

In most instances, the individual image will be shot from the waist up although at times hockey and soccer goalies prefer to have entire body pictures of them, in net.

The pricing below is divided between Beginner, Intermediate, and Expert although because of competition, the expert photographer may be forced to work at beginner prices. Although not considered ethical and in some jurisdictions, illegal, some photographers, to get the contract from a larger organization, will agree to make a donation to that organization or to buy ads in their programs as well as donate toward their banquet. If you must do anything like that to get the work, you'll likely be allowed to charge more.

Additional prints can be charged at the *Add To Order* pricing.

Sitting fees are not common in sport team photography. Since the customer will be filling out the form without you present, you should strive to make the packages and the language on the form as clear and simple as possible with one flat price per package.

Be wary of offering too many packages. Keep it as simple as possible with no more than four price points.

There are many popular things you can add to any of the packages listed below or include them as an option. These include photo buttons, player "bubblegum style cards", photo magnets, and magazine covers. Parents love these things, and often add them to their order.

Package A

Beginner - $75.00 Intermediate $100.00 Expert $125.00

1 - 8x10 group photo

4 - 8x10

4 - 5x7

32 - wallets

Package B

Beginner - $65.00 Intermediate $90.00 Expert $115.00

1 - 8x10 group photo

2 - 8x10

4 - 5x7

24 - wallets

Package C

Beginner - $50.00 Intermediate $75.00 Expert $100.00

1 - 8x10 group photo

2 - 8x10

2 - 5x7

16 - wallets

Package D

Beginner - $35.00 Intermediate $45.00 Expert $55.00

1 - 8x10 group photo

1 - 8x10

2 - 5x7

8 - wallets

Add-Ons

	Beginner	Intermediate	Expert
Photo Buttons*	$5.00	$7.50	$10.00
Player Cards**	12.00	$15.00	$20.00
Photo Magnets***	$5.00	$7.50	$10.00
Magazine Covers****	$7.50	$12.50	$15.00

*Photo Buttons are 3" Round

**Player Cards are a set of 8, double-sided, 2.5"x3.5"

***Photo Magnets are a set of 2, 2.5"x3.5"

****Magazine Covers are 8"x10"

Weddings

Wedding photography is one of the most profitable types of photography and because of that, it's the most competitive -- this is another category that I found the pricing to be all over the place — I found relatively inexperienced photographers with subpar work selling expensive packages, yet at the same time I found talented, experienced photographers underselling their work.

The saturation of the market you're in will be an important factor in how you can structure your pricing — more so then your experience and portfolio strength. With that said, the talented photographer will have no problem getting work — it just might not be at the price point they deserve.

To simplify things, most wedding photographers include a print credit in their packages. I agree that you should be making this as simple and straightforward as possible not only so your prospective customers can fully understand the differences between the packages but so that they, and you, know, precisely what is expected of you and everything you're promising to deliver.

RAW Files - It has now become popular for the prospective client to ask if you'll be giving them the RAW files. I'm not sure how this trend began, but it does come up now and then. Most of the time, the client didn't understand what a RAW file is but was told by one of their friends to, *Make sure the photographer gives you the RAW files!* I highly recommend that you do not ever give your clients the RAW files. Explain to them that the RAW files are unprocessed, computer files that require processing to be properly viewed. Part of what their paying you for is your post processing talents. Explain that in post-production, your signature style is applied to each image. Explain that asking a photographer for the RAW files is like asking the baker for the empty boxes and crates of flour, eggs, nutmeg, etc. that went into making their wedding cake. Flour, eggs, nutmeg and the rest of the ingredients are nothing until the baker uses their talent to create a beautiful and delicious wedding cake. Similarly, the RAW files are nothing until you process them into a beautiful image of a beautiful moment that will be remembered and shared for generations.

Wedding Albums and Books - Wedding prints are often delivered in a wedding album or more common nowadays, in a wedding book. Smaller albums or books for the parents are usually supplied as well. Many photographers have gotten away from including wedding books in their packages but do offer them as an option. The packages I listed do not include albums or books, but pricing for wedding books are included in the *Add To Order* section of this guide. If you would like a package to include wedding books, look up their pricing in the *Add To Order* section and add it to the prices below. I did not include any pricing for albums because the photographer must purchase the cover and pages for the album then assemble it — it's a time-consuming process that is eliminated with the use of wedding books.

Online Gallery - You should have the processed wedding images on an online gallery for your clients to view. I suggest that you make it a public gallery so that not only your clients can view the photos but their parents, relatives, wedding party, and anyone who was at the wedding can view the images provided they have the link. Furthermore, I suggest you watermark the pictures so when they're shared on social media by those involved; you'll get the free advertising. Finally, they should be on an online gallery, such as *SmugMug*, *Zenfolio*, or *PhotoShelter* that allows for ordering -- this will help you to monetize the wedding fully.

Discounts - If wedding photography is seasonal in your area, you may want to give a discount for off-season weddings — I suggest you offer up to a 25% discount for off-season weddings. Also, you may want to offer a discount for any non-Saturday weddings — no matter the season.

Pricing is broken down by *Beginner*, *Intermediate*, and *Expert* and the pricing is for an in-season, Saturday wedding.

Package A

Beginner - $1299.00 Intermediate $1999.00 Expert $3299.00

All Day Coverage (up to 8 hours)

Online gallery for 90-days

75 fully processed images with image release for printing

$150 print credit

Package B

Beginner - $1899.00 Intermediate $2899.00 Expert $4299.00

All Day Coverage (up to 8 hours)

Online gallery for 90-days

100 fully processed images with image release for printing

$150 print credit

Engagement session with 30 digital negatives

Package C
Beginner - $1899.00 Intermediate $2899.00 Expert $4299.00
All Day Coverage (up to 8 hours)
Online gallery for 90-days
150 fully processed images with image release for printing
$200 print credit

Package D
Beginner - $2099.00 Intermediate $3899.00 Expert $5499.00
All Day Coverage (up to 8 hours)
Online gallery for 90-days
200 fully processed images with image release for printing
$200 print credit
Engagement session with 30 digital negatives

Add-Ons
Wedding Rehearsal Coverage
Beginner - $299.00 Intermediate $399.00 Expert $499.00
Up to 2-hours
Up to 2-locations
Online gallery for 90-days
50 fully processed images with image release for printing

Photo Booth
Beginner - $399.00 Intermediate $499.00 Expert $599.00
2-hours coverage after dinner
Fun props, hats, masks, etc provided
Photos are copyright free and supplied on a USB drive
Additional hour of coverage: *Beginner - $100.00 Intermediate $150.00 Expert $200.00*

Add To Order

The product priced here can be sold a la carte or, added to any package of prints and services listed anywhere else in this guide.

Consider the pricing in this section to be very loose. Feel free to adjust it as needed, so it best fits, and compliments, the package your selling.

Pricing is divided by *Beginner*, *Intermediate*, and *Expert* photographers but again, the pricing for this general photography product is very market influenced so you may have to move off these prices to fit your market.

If you must lower a price, try not to let the profit margin for that product drop below 40%.

To calculate profit margin, divide the cost of the product by 1 - (profit margin percentage). So, if something cost you $10.00 and you want to sell it at a 40% profit margin, you would divide $10.00 by (1 - 0.40) where "0.40" is the decimal equivalent of 40% and (1 - 0.40) equals 0.60. $10.00 divided by 0.60 equals $16.67. So, if something costs you $10.00 and you want to sell it at a 40% profit margin, you would sell it for $16.67.

If you want to add Giclée, Canvas, Metal, or Acrylic prints to any package, use the Fine Art pricing for those products.

Beginner

Prints

Unframed, unmounted prints on glossy or satin finish paper.

Wallet (per 8)	$10.00
4x6	$5.00
5x7	$10.00
8x10	$15.00
11x14	$20.00
16x24	$30.00
20x24	$35.00
20x30	$45.00
24x36	$70.00

Digital Only - Fully Processed, Full Size, JPG Images

Distributed via cloud service such as Dropbox or Google Drive. Add $10.00 if you're distributing them by USB drive or CD.

5 JPG's	$25.00
10 JPG's	$30.00
15 JPG's	$35.00
20 JPG's	$40.00
30 JPG's	$50.00
40 JPG's	$60.00

Coffee Table Books

Magazine style paper with cloth covers

5x7 20 Pages	$85.00
8x12 20 Pages	$120.00
11x14 20 Pages	$145.00

*Additional pages are $10.00 each.

Wedding Books

Premium lay-flat books with leather cover for wedding photography and special functions.

5x5 - 10 Pages	$100.00
5x5 - 20 Pages	$130.00
10x8 - 20 Pages	$155.00
10x8 - 30 Pages	$225.00
12x8 - 20 Pages	$155.00
12x8 - 30 Pages	$225.00

*I found the photographer's cost of Wedding Books to vary greatly. I recommend that, as a beginning professional, you take how much the book is costing you to produce, add any shipping then divide that total by 0.60. That will give you a profit margin of 40%.

Photo Cards

Photo cards for holidays, special announcements, and invitations

25 - 4x8 Flat Cards	$40.00
25 - 5x10 Flat Cards	$50.00
25 - 8x10 Flat Cards	$60.00
25 - 4.5x5 Folded Cards	$45.00
25 - 5x7 Folded Cards	$65.00

Miscellaneous Products

Phone Case	$30.00
Phone Skin	$20.00
Photo Buttons	$5.00
3.5x5 Photo Magnets	$7.50
1.6x2.25 Photo Keychain	$20.00

Prints

Unframed, unmounted prints on glossy or satin finish paper.

Wallet (per 8)	$15.00
4x6	$7.50
5x7	$12.50
8x10	$20.00
11x14	$30.00
16x24	$40.00
20x24	$45.00
20x30	$55.00
24x36	$85.00

Digital Only - Fully Processed, Full Size, JPG Images

Distributed via cloud service such as Dropbox or Google Drive. Add $10.00 if you're distributing them by USB drive or CD.

5 JPG's	$30.00
10 JPG's	$35.00
15 JPG's	$40.00
20 JPG's	$45.00
30 JPG's	$60.00
40 JPG's	$70.00

Coffee Table Books

Magazine style paper with cloth covers

5x7 20 Pages	$100.00
8x12 20 Pages	$150.00
11x14 20 Pages	$175.00

*Additional pages are $10.00 each.

Wedding Books

Premium lay-flat books with leather cover for wedding photography and special functions.

5x5 - 10 Pages	$120.00
5x5 - 20 Pages	$155.00
10x8 - 20 Pages	$185.00
10x8 - 30 Pages	$270.00
12x8 - 20 Pages	$185.00
12x8 - 30 Pages	$270.00

*I found the photographer's cost of Wedding Books to vary greatly. I recommend that, as an intermediate professional, you take how much the book is costing you to produce, add any shipping then divide that total by 0.50. That will give you a profit margin of 50%.

Photo Cards

Photo cards for holidays, special announcements, and invitations

25 - 4x8 Flat Cards	$45.00
25 - 5x10 Flat Cards	$55.00
25 - 8x10 Flat Cards	$65.00
25 - 4.5x5 Folded Cards	$50.00
25 - 5x7 Folded Cards	$70.00

Miscellaneous Products

Phone Case	$35.00
Phone Skin	$25.00
Photo Buttons	$7.50
3.5x5 Photo Magnets	$10.00
1.6x2.25 Photo Keychain	$25.00

Prints

Unframed, unmounted prints on glossy or satin finish paper.

Wallet (per 8)	$20.00
4x6	$10.00
5x7	$15.00
8x10	$25.00
11x14	$35.00
16x24	$45.00
20x24	$50.00
20x30	$60.00
24x36	$90.00

Digital Only - Fully Processed, Full Size, JPG Images

Distributed via cloud service such as Dropbox or Google Drive. Add $10.00 if you're distributing them by USB drive or CD.

5 JPG's	$35.00
10 JPG's	$40.00
15 JPG's	$45.00
20 JPG's	$50.00
30 JPG's	$65.00
40 JPG's	$75.00

Coffee Table Books

Magazine style paper with cloth covers

5x7 20 Pages	$125.00
8x12 20 Pages	$175.00
11x14 20 Pages	$200.00

*Additional pages are $20.00 each.

Wedding Books

Premium lay-flat books with leather cover for wedding photography and special functions.

5x5 - 10 Pages	$150.00
5x5 - 20 Pages	$190.00
10x8 - 20 Pages	$230.00
10x8 - 30 Pages	$335.00
12x8 - 20 Pages	$230.00
12x8 - 30 Pages	$335.00

*I found the photographer's cost of Wedding Books to vary greatly. I recommend that, as an expert professional, you take how much the book is costing you to produce, add any shipping then divide that total by 0.40. That will give you a profit margin of 60%.

Photo Cards

Photo cards for holidays, special announcements, and invitations

25 - 4x8 Flat Cards	$50.00
25 - 5x10 Flat Cards	$60.00
25 - 8x10 Flat Cards	$70.00
25 - 4.5x5 Folded Cards	$55.00
25 - 5x7 Folded Cards	$75.00

Miscellaneous Products

Phone Case	$40.00
Phone Skin	$30.00
Photo Buttons	$10.00
3.5x5 Photo Magnets	$15.00
1.6x2.25 Photo Keychain	$30.00

Did You Like The 2019 Guide to Pricing Your Photography?

Before you go, I'd like to say "thank you" for purchasing my guide. I know you could have picked from dozens of books and visited dozens of websites on how to price your photography, but you took a chance with my book. So a big thanks for buying this book and reading all the way to the end. Now I'd like to ask for a *small* favor. Could you please take a minute or two and leave a review for this book on Amazon? This feedback will help me continue to write the kind of books that help you get results. And if you loved it, then please let me know :-)

Tony@AnthonyMorganti.com

Finally, if you'd like to learn more about photography, from the click of the shutter to post-processing, please visit my website — I add to it daily:

https://OnlinePhotographyTraining.com

About The Author

"Quality Photography Training Shouldn't Break the Bank"

Most of the so-called 'photography gurus' provide just enough free and low-priced content to reel you into purchasing their expensive, in-depth courses. Many cannot afford those higher priced courses, stalling their photography training.

Anthony Morganti became known providing quality, free, videos on YouTube and his website, OnlinePhotographyTraining.com. All his videos are free -- nearly 900 with several more being created every week.

Anthony writes books to supplement his free video content, or to teach a difficult subject, the best way possible. Like everything Anthony does, his training is most affordable -- with most of his books costing no more than a cup of coffee, you'll enjoy Anthony's concise, no-nonsense approach to teaching photography.

Anthony's studio is located in the historic Ellicott Square Building in downtown Buffalo.

In his spare time, Anthony likes to travel, spend time with his family and, what else? Take pictures!

www.ingramcontent.com/pod-product-compliance
Lightning Source LLC
Chambersburg PA
CBHW062335220526

45469CB00008B/2722